ESSENTIAL
LENT

ESSENTIAL
LENT

Holy Moments and Sacred Experiences for Your Whole Congregation

Aimée J. Jannsohn, Editor

Open Waters Publishing
700 Prospect Avenue
Cleveland, Ohio 44115
www.openwaterspublishing.com

Aimée J. Jannsohn, editor
Design by Robyn Henderson Nordstrom

Printed in the United States of America

First Edition: January 2014

10 9 8 7 6 5 4 3 2 1

Open Waters Publishing is an imprint of The Pilgrim Press.
The Open Waters Publishing name and logo are trademarks
of Local Church Ministries, the United Church of Christ.

ISBN 978-0-8298-2000-3

CONTENTS

Activities for Younger Children (Ages 3-6)

Activities for Intergenerational Groups

Activities for Seekers and Those New to Church

Worship Resources for Lent, Holy Week, and Easter

FOREWORD

You have six weeks to experience Lent, the most sacred season of the church year. During that short time—from the solemn beginnings of Ash Wednesday to the trumpets on Easter morning—Lent must seep in, be absorbed, and live within your congregation.

The activities in *Essential Lent* have been crafted for every age group and individual faith journey you'll find at your church: children, youth, adults, intergenerational groups—even seekers and those who have recently begun attending your services.

And speaking of services, the worship resources here will honor the rituals and traditions of the Church during this holy season as well as introduce some new ways to observe Lent, Holy Week, and Easter.

It's true, Lent resources can be found in many Christian education materials and curricula—pages and pages of the same lessons, year after year. *Essential Lent* is a fresh Lent experience that invites your faith community to walk with Jesus during his final days, through scripture, prayer, crafts, service, art, drama, music, food, fellowship, and more. All in one volume.

So, prepare to
pray...
act...
serve...
worship...
reflect...
sing...
create...
learn...
bake...
eat...
and ultimately, celebrate the risen Christ!

Let the Lenten journey begin.

Aimée J. Jannsohn, editor

ACTIVITIES FOR
ADULTS

The activities in this chapter will be most meaningful
for adults who are active in the life of your
congregation and knowledgeable about the seasons of
the church year, especially Lent and Easter.

YEAR-ROUND
EASTER HOSPITALITY

Leader preparation: If your congregation uses the Lectionary for worship, this will be a teachable moment to reinforce that practice. Read through the activity and consider ways you might enable connections between it and the practices of your congregation.

Supplies:

- Bibles
- paper and pencils

Ask volunteers to read aloud John 13:1–7, 31b–35 and Acts 2:42–47. Have the group identify ways that hospitality is given or received in each passage. Form two groups. Assign one scripture passage to each group. Challenge each group to create a presentation that convinces the other group that their passage makes the best case to view hospitality as a legitimate, year-round practice for any disciple. If time permits, reverse the passages and have each group make a case for the other passage.

Ask each group to create a bulletin announcement to be used at the beginning of each church season that lifts up hospitality based on scripture as a practice of faithful discipleship. Reminder: The church seasons and liturgical colors are Advent (blue or purple), Christmas/Christmastide (white), Epiphany (green), Lent (purple), Holy Week and Pentecost (red), and Ordinary time (green). Plan how these announcements might be used in your congregation.

RESURRECTION PROCESS

Leader preparation: Take a clump of modeling clay and make a cross or other faith-related object that has some significance. Think about stories, scripture, or people of which this icon reminds you. Hold it in your hand and say this or a similar prayer: *Dear God, we are the Easter people. We are followers of your wonderful cross. Bless me as I strive to let go of what needs releasing and walk confidently into what requires my gifts and my ministry. Amen.*

Supplies:
- modeling clay
- paper and pens or pencils

The cross symbolizes the Christian faith and walk. Other symbols may touch believers as much as or more than the cross. These symbols enliven our faith and help us think about its relevance in our lives today. The cross, a towel, a fish, a dove, and the bread and cup are all personal and communal doorways to the paradox of life and death, right here and now. When we die to the old, we step into the new, ready or not, happily or reluctantly. People sometimes fear change. At times we all cling to the past. To die to the old takes courage and a willingness to act. It also takes letting go of the ego and the need to know or be right about everything.

Invite the group to take a clump of clay and hold it for a few moments with their eyes closed. Then, with their eyes open, have them mold a symbol that has great meaning for them. Take time to let each one share with the group his or her creation and its significance. Has anyone gained new insight or direction during this exercise? Anything they need to let go of? Have them share that as well.

EASTER ANYTIME

Leader preparation: Easter in October or July or January? We celebrate Easter anytime and read Easter texts because Easter is the meaning of Sunday worship. Try "celebrating" Easter in October, for instance, to see how important it is to separate its meaning from the bulbs, buds, new clothes, and springtime imagery, and to understand how southern hemisphere Christians perceive Easter as Christ being the first fruit of God's harvest. We celebrate Easter as the message of future and vision because ultimately, it's our most transforming and welcoming message.

Supplies:
- Bible
- (optional) bunny ears for the leader

Share the statement about Easter anytime in the preceding paragraph. Join in the following gathering litany, inviting members of the group to improvise and contribute the "no matters . . ."

Leader: No matter who you are, no matter where you are on life's journey, you are welcome here!

Group: And so are you!

Leader: No matter if you're old or young, male or female—

Group: You are welcome to Easter!

Leader: No matter your racial or ethnic background—

Group: You are welcome to Easter!

Leader: No matter your sexual orientation or your abilities—

Group: You are welcome to Easter!

Leader: No matter . . .*(have the group fill in)*

Group: You are welcome to Easter!

Leader: No matter . . .*(have the group fill in)*

Group: You are welcome to Easter!

Prayer of Confession: *Gracious God, we confess that we think of Easter as the "springtime holiday" rather than the mystery holiday, the hope-time holiday, the now-it's-up-to-us holiday. We're more at home with bulbs and bunnies than mortality and resurrection. We confess that we're afraid to talk about death and we avoid those who are dying or leave their tender care to others. We confess that sometimes we engage in personal and community behaviors that are life-denying. Sometimes we let things die—hopes and dreams, relationships, communities of faith—because we aren't willing to claim your tomb-opening power. Accept our repentance and be risen in each of our lives. Amen.*

Assurance of Grace: *Christ, who is more loving than can be contained in any holiday, ritual, or sanctuary, forgives our sins and changes our hearts. Christ doesn't give us new shoes, but a new way to walk. Amen.*

Ask a volunteer to read aloud Mark 16:1–8. The story goes that Rev. R. W. Dale, a pastor in Birmingham, England, at the turn of the 19th century, was stuck one year in his Easter sermon until he realized that the phrase "Christ is living" had never really meant anything to him except "Christ was living way back then, died way back then, and was resurrected way back then." He figured his congregation didn't really believe it either, so he decided to sing an Easter hymn every Sunday until he was sure they understood. His congregation was still singing "Alleluia" when he retired from the ministry many years later.

Discuss how the group feels about celebrating Easter in a season other than spring, even every week. (Each Sunday, after all, is a "little Easter.") What would the congregation think of an "Easter in October" service with pumpkins and apples instead of lilies? How would they respond if every week's worship service included some kind of affirmation of Easter?

SWING INTO SPRING

Leader preparation: Playful elements of the resurrection may challenge some in your group. Reflect prayerfully and personally on the deep joy of the resurrection and the promise it gives to life—within and beyond life on earth.

Supplies:

- handout: *Swing into Spring, a Latvian Easter Tradition*, page 17
- plastic Easter eggs
- Mark 16:1–8 (Cut up verse by verse without verse numbers; fold in Easter eggs hidden around the room.)
- more plastic eggs containing single words: *hope, life, risen, Christ, Alleluia, is, mystery, no, death, blessing, good news, joy.* (Repeat words as many times as necessary so that everyone gets to find an egg.)

Invite the group to hunt for Easter eggs until everyone has one (or two, if there are extras). Explain that although Easter egg hunts are a playful part of Easter, the eggs have come from earlier religions as symbols of fertility and new growth, like lilies and rabbits. They're not a part of the faith story, but rather, are parables. The butterfly with its three-fold life is also often used as a parable. Have those who found eggs with scripture verses read them in the order they think is correct. (If the order is only slightly inaccurate, there's no need to correct them.) There may be a sense of surprise; verse 8 stands out when the text is read this way. Explain that it's the original ending in this first gospel, and that most scholars agree that the latter verses were added at a much later date.

Distribute *Swing into Spring, a Latvian Easter Tradition* by Indulis Gleske. In Latvia, the Easter "play" custom is swinging. Discuss ways in which Jesus' resurrection, as Gleske suggests, involves a letting go of gravity, a trusting of the fulcrum and—not least—a thrilling ride.

Invite the group into a time of prayer. Ask if anyone knows of somebody who has died in the past year and given over his or her place on this earth's swing, so to speak. Name these people, and ask those who found single words in their Easter eggs to read them aloud one at a time, in any order they choose, transforming the words into a prayer.

SWING INTO SPRING,
A LATVIAN EASTER TRADITION

The northerly country of Latvia, located on the Baltic Sea, experiences large changes in the position of the sun during the year, and the spiritual customs are very much based on the passage of the sun. The Spring Equinox traditionally was called "Big Day," but pre-Christian equinox customs now have become associated with Easter.

One of the traditional rituals of this occasion is the hanging of swings, large and small, in towns and in the country. Swings can be as simple as a single board suspended by ropes from a tree branch, or more complex structures with solid frameworks to carry several people. The swings can be erected in a town square, or anywhere, for that matter. Ready-made swing sets, sturdy structures of bolted together logs, are available for instant rental and deployment in house yards or parking lots.

It is expected that swinging will bring good crops, and no doubt is an aid to courtship, as young men take young women for rides, showing off their prowess at driving the swings higher and higher. All ages get to ride, as children or older folks are taken as passengers on larger swings.

The swing, like other symbols of the passage of seasons or stages of our lives, is governed by laws of nature. Its timeframe has to do with distance from the fulcrum to the center of gravity, and we cannot change that. We get on the swing, and someone gives a gentle shove to start us off. We slightly manipulate the center of gravity by shifting our weight, and make the swing go higher and higher, until we see over the onlookers or the treetops, and feel the excitement, the thrill, and even trepidation as we hang on to the ropes or the frame.

Eventually, we slow down, come to a stop. We relinquish our place to the next couple, and give them a gentle push to start off . . .

For Christians, this time of life's renewal is marked by the resurrection of Jesus, and as the old customs of Latvia merged with the new, the Easter observation appropriately took on the name of "Big Day."

by Indulis Gleske, From the book *Gifts in Open Hands: More Worship Resources for the Global Community*, edited by Maren Tirabassi and Kathy Wonson Eddy (Cleveland: The Pilgrim Press)

ACTIVITIES FOR
YOUNG ADULTS

The following activities focusing on Lenten practices
and rituals will engage these plugged-in multi-taskers,
whether they grew up in the church or are seeking a
faith community.

ASHES TO ASHES

Leader preparation: It's a good idea to prepare the ashes for this activity in advance. If you have palm leaves on hand from the previous Lenten season, burn them to create the ash. If not, simply burn some dried leaves or paper. Grind the ashes into a powder. Mix together in a small bowl with a few drops of olive or mineral oil so ashes will adhere to the skin. Be sure the artwork on the supplies list is easily visible to the entire group.

Supplies:

- ashes
- small bowl
- artwork: "Out of Work" by Käthe Kollwitz, found on Google Images

Take time to look together at "Out of Work." Ask the group what they notice about the images and what catches their attention. What connection do these images have with the spiritual practice of honoring the body? What stages of life are represented? Christian tradition acknowledges that the body is finite, bound by time and—ultimately—decay. When we're young we often ignore this reality. Why might that be? How does our understanding of our own finitude affect (positively or negatively) how we treat our own bodies and others' bodies? Consider together the attitudes the surrounding culture has to the body's finitude. Invite the group to consider how these attitudes compare to those found in the church. (If you wish, extend this activity by making the ashes together. Give each person a slip of paper and invite them to write a few sentences expressing how they feel about the finitude of their own bodies. Burn these slips of paper together to make the ashes for this activity.)

When ready, participate together in the Christian tradition of the imposition of ashes, which symbolizes both repentance of sin and the relative shortness of our earthly lives. Take turns putting your thumb in the ashes and making the sign of a small cross on someone's forehead while repeating the phrase: "Remember that you are dust and to dust you will return."

STATIONS OF THE CROSS WALK

Leader preparation: Taking a pilgrimage to holy sites is an ancient tradition in many faiths. One classic pilgrimage for Christians is traveling to Jerusalem and walking the path of Jesus as he was sent to death on the cross. This activity invites young adults to walk with Jesus and see Jesus in their own context. It may occur at any time, but is particularly suited for Lent or Good Friday. You may even wish to establish it as a new ritual for your congregation.

To learn more about the Stations of the Cross, visit the website "The Voice: Biblical and Theological Resources for Growing Christians" at *www.crivoice.org/stations.html*. Consider them within your local community. Identify eight places where significant or ordinary events have taken place in the neighborhood surrounding your church. Use "A Service of Stations of the Cross" for the scripture passages and any other elements of worship you would like to use.

Write a brief description of the event or the significance of the place in your neighborhood as a site of healing or gathering, or as a source of pain or injustice. Pair each of the eight places with a station of the cross. If possible, design the route to begin and end at your church. Invite young adults from other churches in the area and, if you wish, members of all ages to join your group on the cross walk.

Supplies:

- Bibles or copies of "A Service of Stations of the Cross" from *www.crivoice.org/stations.html*
- eight "stations" for your cross walk and brief descriptions of each place

On the appointed day, gather with young adults and others who wish to participate to walk the stations of cross. At each place pause for a time to read about the place, to meditate on the meaning of the place or the events that transpired there, and to hear the scripture pertaining to the station. Move on until all the stations are completed. Invite everyone to conclude with silent meditations or prayers for healing and justice in your community. Depart in silence.

PRETZEL PRAYERS

Leader preparation: Think about what you do when someone says: "Let us pray." Do you reflexively bow your head and fold your hands? While this is a common prayer posture, it's not the only one. In medieval times, Christians often prayed by crossing their arms over their chests while standing or sitting. In this activity you and your group of young adults will have the opportunity to practice this prayer posture.

Legend has it that medieval monks made pretzels to teach this prayer posture. The pretzels were made from a simple recipe of flour, water, and salt and eaten during Lent, as they contained no leaven. The simplicity of the dough and the prayer shape reminded people to pray and ask God's forgiveness during Lent. Similarly, the three holes created by twisting the dough can be used to explain the Trinity, in which God is at once Father (or Mother, Parent, etc.), Son, and Holy Spirit.

For this activity, you'll need to gather ingredients ahead of time and arrange to meet in a kitchen to bake together. It's recommended that you prepare a batch of pretzels in advance as practice for the group activity. Enjoy learning to pray in a new "old" way and share in a simple snack. This is also a good activity for discussing Lent and its rituals throughout history and in your faith community.

Supplies:
- Bible
- recipe: Lenten Pretzels, page 23, one copy per person
- ingredients and supplies to make pretzels (see recipe)
- water or other beverages to drink with the snack
- (optional) mustard or melted cheese for toppings

Gather in the kitchen. Ask the group to name different postures for prayer, such as kneeling, bowing heads, hand raised above head, hands open facing up, and folded hands. Explain that there's no right or wrong way to pray. Tell them that throughout the history of Christianity as well as other faiths people have prayed in different ways. One such way is to fold hands across one's chest. Practice this posture. Invite the group to stand, cross their arms over their chests, and allow their hands to rest flat near their shoulders. Explain that this posture reminds us that God enfolds us and encircles us always. While in this posture, lead the young adults in praying Jesus' Prayer together: "Lord Jesus Christ, Son of God, have mercy on me, the sinner."

Tell the group that, according to folklore, monks in the Middle Ages used pretzels as a teaching tool to remind people to pray and seek forgiveness during Lent, and used the prayer posture that they've just practiced. Follow the recipe and work together to make pretzels. Suggest to the group that they consider establishing a new tradition of having a pretzel-making party at church or at home every year to mark the season of Lent. Enjoy a snack of pretzels and beverages, and close with a prayer of thanksgiving, using the crossed-arm posture. Give each person a copy of the pretzel recipe to take home.

LENTEN PRETZELS

Ingredients (makes 12 pretzels)

Soda solution:

1/3 cup baking soda   5 cups water

Pretzel dough:

1½ cups all-purpose flour   1½ cups wheat flour

1 teaspoon baking soda   1 cup buttermilk

¼ cup honey

2 tablespoons kosher salt for tops of pretzels

Instructions:

- Preheat oven to 400 degrees.
- Dissolve soda and water in a stock pot and bring to a boil. Remove from heat and set aside.
- Sift together flour and soda. Add buttermilk and honey, stirring until dough pulls together.
- Pour dough onto a lightly floured surface and knead until firm.
- Divide dough into 12 equal pieces. Roll each into a long, snake-like piece and form traditional pretzel twist shape.
- Pinch the ends to seal it and dip pretzel in soda-water solution.
- Place on lightly greased baking sheet and sprinkle with kosher salt.
- Bake in the oven for 10 minutes or until golden brown. Move to a cooling rack for a few minutes before eating.

PRAYING WITHOUT CEASING: 24-HOUR VIGIL MEET-UP

Leader preparation: This activity can take place within your faith community. It can be low-tech using the supplies listed, or your young adults may decide to expand the participant base to your local community or beyond that, to include surrounding communities. This activity is for a low-tech, local version. The vigil can occur during any season, but works particularly well in the 24-hour period of Good Friday or Holy Saturday, leading the group into the joy of Easter.

Arrange to use a chapel or sanctuary for this time of prayer. In the weeks leading up to the vigil, you'll need to enlist the help of six "prayer captains," each of whom will take one four-hour shift, ensure that those praying are safe (especially necessary for the overnight hours), and that supplies are readily available.

Other versions of the vigil: Conduct via Facebook (or other social networking site), having each person sign in to a page created for the group at their appointed hour. They pray from home and enter traditional Christian prayers or prayers from scripture onto the page. Another alternative is to create a "meet-up" on the Web. Coordinate with young adult groups from other local churches to meet up at a park or common site for a mass prayer service in which a large group of people can gather to pray their prayers together.

Create a sign-up sheet with 24 one-hour slots. Before the activity begins, the young adults will need to gather to prepare the space.

Supplies:
- sign-up sheet with 24 spaces marked for each hour
- table with covering
- several chairs (comfortable, if possible)
- (optional) reading lamp
- Bibles, in several different translations
- cross or other Christian symbols

- tissues

- paper and pens

- devotional materials: prayer books, devotionals, religious art or photographs of nature

- candles and matches

- small clock

- water, coffee, tea

- cups

- six prayer captains

- recordings of meditative or spiritual music

- music player

Invite the young adults to sign up to participate in a 24-hour prayer vigil. Explain that the group will need to gather to set up the space in advance. Tell them that when they come for the vigil, they can use their hour in prayer however they wish. Let them know there will be Bibles in several different translations, devotional materials, paper, pens, and music available to use. If they choose, they can sit quietly or try different ways to pray. Point out which entrance to use and let them know who the prayer captains will be throughout the vigil.

About 30 minutes before the vigil is scheduled to begin, invite the group to set up the chapel or sanctuary. Set up the table with the Bibles, paper, pens, devotional materials, candles, matches, a cross or other Christian symbols, and a box of tissues. On one sheet of paper, write the heading "Prayer Requests" and begin a list with several prayer concerns from the group. Place a small clock where it's visible, but not distracting. Set up a reading lamp, if necessary. Provide one or two chairs, preferably comfortable ones. Set up a place for coffee, tea, and water. Gather the group and offer a prayer for them, the vigil, and the volunteers who are giving their time to be present throughout this event. Tell the group that when they come for their designated time, they should greet one another with these words: "The peace of Christ be with you."

ACTIVITIES FOR
YOUTH
(AGES 12-17)

These Lent and Easter activities will nurture faith development as they bring youth of all ages together in a supportive team environment.

GUATEMALA: PROCESSION PART 1

Leader preparation: Different cultures celebrate high holy days in different ways. What may seem exhausting and a lot of work to one may feel like reprieve and relaxation to another. Do an Internet search for "Semana Santa" and learn what some other cultures do during Holy Week. Other searches might include "Holy Week," "processions," etc.

Supplies:

- artwork: "Guatemala: Procession" by Betty LaDuke, found on Google Images

For most Christians, Holy Week is a time to reflect on our spiritual journeys. We begin with Palm Sunday and end on Easter with some sort of celebration, some more elaborate than others. Share with youth what you have learned from studying Holy Week celebrations in other cultures. Look at the artwork "Guatemala: Procession." Try to bring out all of the images you see in the picture. Think about the work that might be involved for an elaborate Holy Week procession.

GUATEMALA: PROCESSION PART 2

Leader preparation: Have the artwork "Guatemala: Procession" by Betty LaDuke available to share with youth. Collect a variety of magazines that can be cut up and used.

Supplies:
- artwork: "Guatemala: Procession" by Betty LaDuke, found on Google Images
- computer with Internet and projection capability
- images of Holy Week processions in Guatemala, found on Google Images
- magazines
- colored paper
- scissors
- glue

Guatemala has some of the most beautiful Holy Week celebrations in the world. The processions are colorful and elaborate. Show the group the artwork and images of the celebrations. What do they notice in both? What are other church celebrations they have heard of or seen that are filled with color and beauty? What made those celebrations particularly spectacular—the people, the display, the colors, the costumes, the music? How do these large-scale activities relate to faith?

If the group were going to celebrate a story or passage from scripture, which story would it be? Have youth work with a partner or in small groups to choose a Bible story they would turn into a large, spectacular procession. It can be any story or passage from the Old or New Testament—Moses, Garden of Eden, creation, Christmas, or the Magi. Which colors would they use? Which style of art? Who would be involved? Where would the celebration take place?

Option: Suggest to youth that they create art in the style of "Guatemala: Procession" that depicts a scene from scripture.

FOOT WASHING

Leader preparation: Because this activity is based around Holy Thursday (or Maundy Thursday), you may wish to read an article about this holy day on Wikipedia or another reference website. It may prove helpful in case any specific questions arise regarding the history and practice of this day and the foot-washing ritual. Prepare the worship space by placing a chair and footstool in the center of the room with a pillow nearby for kneeling. Next to the pillow, place a large bowl of water that contains a small amount of dish soap. Near the water, place one small towel for each person. Obtain a musical recording of the song, "Wash, O God, Our Sons and Daughters."

Supplies:
- Bible
- chair
- pillow for kneeling
- bowl of water
- dish soap
- small towel for each person
- musical recording of "Wash, O God, Our Sons and Daughters" OR
- music player or computer with Internet, if playing from YouTube

Invite youth to sit in a circle with the chair and basin in the center. Read aloud John 13:1–15. Jesus washed his disciples' feet in order to set an example for them. In Jesus' day feet were particularly dirty and the act was very symbolic. Jesus' act told the disciples that they should be servants to the world around them. Though the disciples were the students and Jesus their Lord, Jesus washed their feet as a servant might do. When Jesus finished, he instructed the disciples to go and do likewise. Many churches continue this ritual by offering a special foot washing service on Thursday of Holy Week, because that's when Jesus washed his disciples' feet. Suggest that because it's hands rather than feet that usually get dirty, they'll be washing hands. Tell the group that as a disciple of Jesus, they will begin the ritual by washing one of their hands. Then, in turn, each person will wash the hands of another person.

Play and repeat the song "Wash, O God, Our Sons and Daughters" throughout this ritual. Invite one person to sit in the chair. Kneel down and gently wash this person's hands and dry them with a towel. Then have them kneel and invite the next person to come to the chair. Repeat this pattern until everyone's hands have been washed. Close by saying, "Disciples! How will you serve the world around you? Go and do so!"

CASCARONES BLESSINGS

Leader preparation: Count your blessings, and look forward to a time of laughter and fun with your youth by making *cascarones*. Cut a circle 1" in diameter in one end of each raw egg by pricking the shell with a needle or cake tester. Carefully remove the small circle of eggshell, discard it, and pour out the egg. Save the eggs for cake or omelets. Wash the shells and put them back in the egg carton for drying and transport.

Supplies:

- two eggs for each youth, plus a few extras that are hollowed out, washed, and dry
- tissue paper in bright colors
- birdseed or rice, enough to fill each eggshell about halfway
- funnels (not essential, but helpful for pouring seeds into eggshells)
- tape for resealing *cascarones*
- felt-tip markers
- Bible, marked at 1 Peter 3:8–9

Ask the group to share ideas about what the word "blessing" means. Hand out sets of scripture blessings, and invite youth to read them aloud. Explore the following topic with your group: If God is the source of blessing, how does it make sense for us to bless one another? (Possible answers: We bless one another to be reminded of God's blessing. We serve as channels for the grace and mercy of God by offering blessings to one another. When we bless a stranger or an enemy, we change the dynamic of our relationship.) Remind your group that sharing God's blessing doesn't always require spoken words. Blessings can be channeled through acts of joy, laughter, and kindness. Conclude your discussion by asking someone to read aloud 1 Peter 3:8-9.

Explain that "*cascarone*" means eggshell in Spanish. *Cascarones* are used as party favors at Easter and other holiday times. *Cascarones* bring laughter, good luck, and blessings to those around us. The first *cascarone* will be shared today with someone in your group. The second is for youth to take with them so they can offer a surprise blessing to anyone they choose.

Have each person fill and decorate two eggs. For each egg, choose a word of blessing to write on the outside of the egg. Then fill the eggs with birdseed or rice and reseal the eggshell by taping a couple of layers of tissue paper over the opening. Don't cover the entire egg with paper, or it won't crack open later. After the egg is sealed, decorate it using felt-tip markers.

Once all the *cascarones* are filled and decorated, go outside to a grassy place where birds can enjoy the birdseed from the *cascarones*. Now the fun begins. Crush them in your hand, while cracking them gently on one another's heads. Stand in a circle so that everyone can crack their egg over the head of the person to their left, or randomly choose recipients. Remind everyone to read and enjoy their blessings amid the chaos. Sweep up extra seeds if necessary. Have youth take home their extra *cascarone* as a surprise for someone else.

WHAT'S NEXT? LOW SUNDAY OR SECOND SUNDAY OF EASTER

Leader preparation: This activity works best on "Low Sunday," most commonly referred to as the Second Sunday of Easter. After the death of Jesus and before the experience of the resurrection, the disciples and the community at large were in a lull. The Messiah had died. Whether or not one was a follower of Jesus, no one could deny that the past days had been filled with excitement and activity. Now that Jesus was dead and the crowds had dispersed, for many, it was back to business as usual. That might have felt mundane and boring in comparison.

Both Joseph of Arimathea and the authorities were concerned about what to do with the body of Jesus, but for different reasons. Joseph, out of respect, wanted to place the body in a tomb to offer a proper burial. The authorities, afraid of the rumors of a resurrection, wanted to make sure the body was secure in the tomb. This was an unsettling time as the disciples tried to understand what had just happened and what was next . . . if anything.

Supplies:
- Bibles or copies of Matthew 27:51–66
- construction paper, markers, pens, stickers, ribbons, glitter, etc.
- list of people in your church who are grieving

The disciples are used to following Jesus around, preaching, teaching, telling the gospel. Now that he's dead, what are they to do? What message will they bear now? They haven't heard about the resurrection yet. They're afraid they, too, may be killed. They're trying to figure out what the last three years have meant in light of what has occurred over the past few days.

Invite youth to think about their memories of church traditions on Palm Sunday. Some churches have confirmations or baptisms on that day; others may have big processionals with palms and fanfare. Encourage them to think about the rest of Holy Week, especially the Saturday before Easter. What are those days like? Are they hectic? Do they feel empty compared to Palm Sunday and Easter Sunday? Invite them to think about what those days might be like if we didn't know to celebrate Easter, if we didn't know what to expect next. In many churches, the Sunday after Easter is referred to as Low Sunday, as the church feels empty after being so full and busy on Easter Sunday.

Relate this to the experience of losing a loved one. From the time of death to the funeral, the mourners are busy preparing, making funeral arrangements, picking out flowers and caskets, notifying family and friends. There's usually a time of visitation at the funeral home in which people come to express their sympathy. A meal is often served following the funeral, where people gather and tell stories of the deceased. Then everyone goes home. Ask the youth to think about how this might feel to the family left behind, especially if it's a spouse whose children are grown. This may seem like too much rest to the people who are mourning.

Read the list you gathered of those in your church who are grieving. Plan to make a greeting card for them that will remind them that the church is still there for them. If possible, plan a time for the group to pay them a visit. Before you go, help youth find the right words to say so they don't feel awkward.

ACTIVITIES FOR
OLDER
CHILDREN
(AGES 7-11)

The following activities will invite older children to participate more fully in the life of the church by exploring significant rituals and traditions during Lent and Easter.

CELEBRATING THE SEASONS

Leader preparation: The church year is filled with celebrations in which we bring out our best and dress up our worship. Many churches decorate with banners and flowers at Christmas and Easter, but what other times in the church year can we bring out the beauty of the season and enhance our space? If possible, talk with the person in charge of your worship space and ask if your group can plan to prepare the space in a special way for one of the upcoming Sundays.

Supplies:

- markers and newsprint or whiteboard
- "Seasons of the Church Year," page 39
- Bible

Ask the children to list some seasons of the church year; refer to "Seasons of the Church Year," page 39.

If your church has altar cloths, talk about the different colors of the cloths that are used for each season and what symbols they might have on them. Do people order special flowers for certain days or times of the year? Are banners hung in your sanctuary for certain occasions?

What other decorations do you remember using at different times of the church year? Think about the coming Sundays. Is there a Sunday on which your group would like to prepare the worship space in a special way?

Invite the children to create a paper banner that could form the basis for the development of a cloth banner. Read Psalm 8, and make that the theme of their banner. These questions may help guide your project:

- In what season of the church year will this Sunday fall?
- What scripture will you feature? (If your pastor follows the Revised Common Lectionary, ask which texts will be used on the Sunday you've chosen.)
- What colors will you use? Why?
- What images would you want on the banner? How will those images help the congregation understand the worship theme that day?

Option: If there are people in your congregation who sew, see if they would be willing to create a cloth banner from the children's paper banner.

SEASONS OF THE CHURCH YEAR

SEASON	COLOR	LENGTH
Advent	Blue/Purple	4 weeks before Dec. 25
Christmas	White	12 days
Epiphany	White or Green	7-9 weeks, depends on the date of Easter
Lent	Purple	6 weeks
Easter/Eastertide	White/Gold	50 days
Pentecost Day	Red	1 Sunday
Season after Pentecost, or Ordinary Time	Green	After Pentecost until Advent

SOME SPECIAL DAYS TO CONSIDER DURING THESE SEASONS:

Advent
Blue Christmas service (Resources can be found on Google by searching for "Blue Christmas Service.")

Epiphany
Baptism of Jesus
   (first Sunday after Epiphany)
Transfiguration
   (last Sunday after Epiphany)

Lent
Ash Wednesday
Palm Sunday/Passion Sunday
Holy Thursday (Maundy Thursday)
Good Friday

Easter

Season After Pentecost
Pentecost Sunday
Trinity Sunday
   (first Sunday after Pentecost)
World Communion Sunday
   (first Sunday in October)
Reign of Christ Sunday
   (last Sunday after Pentecost)

SOME OTHER DATES TO CONSIDER
(Check with your denomination to see when these are celebrated and what resources are available.)

New Year's Day (Some churches have a special celebration on this day.)

Martin Luther King Jr. Day
   (or closest Sunday)

Health and Human Service Sunday

Racial Justice Sunday

Church Vocations Sunday

Amistad Sunday

Pacific Islander and Asian American
   Ministries Sunday

Mother's Day

Father's Day

Christian Education Sunday

American Indian Ministry Sunday

Access and Disabilities Sunday

Children's Sabbath

Higher Education Sunday

Laity Sunday

Stewardship Sunday

LENT AND EASTER RITUALS

Leader preparation: What are the different rituals your church observes around Lent and Easter? What items would serve as reminders of each of these rituals? Gather supplies and place them in a box or bag to keep them out of sight.

Supplies:
- items that will remind the group of Lent and Easter rituals, such as an Easter lily or Easter egg
- box or bag to hold items
- paper and pencils

Ask your group to think about the different rituals that take place in your church around Lent and Easter. One by one, bring out the related items. Have someone keep track of the rituals. How do these rituals help us to share the stories of our faith? In what ways do they help us better understand our faith? How can they help us explain our faith to others? Decorate your space with something for Lent and Easter.

THE LAST SUPPER

Leader preparation: Gather supplies. Read Mark 14:22–25. Cut out "question mark" shapes from paper. Be prepared to help younger children write their questions, or have them dictate to an older child.

Supplies:
- Bibles
- small loaf of bread, cup, grape juice
- Bible story books depicting the Last Supper
- paper "question marks," pencils, erasers
- bread or crackers, grapes or juice, napkins

Warmly welcome the children. Make introductions if there are newcomers. Invite the children to read aloud Mark 14:22–25. As you read, dramatize the story by holding up bread and a cup of grape juice. After the story invite the children's reflections. Show them various art images of the Last Supper. Imagine how the disciples might have felt as they shared this meal with Jesus. What might they have been feeling, thinking, wondering? We aren't the first to experience questions, joys, and sorrows. Give the children the "question marks" and invite them to write their questions to God. Then serve the bread and grapes or juice. Remind them that the Lord's Supper is a special meal for all God's children. It strengthens us, as God's people, to love and serve others.

SEMANA SANTA

Leader preparation: In Central America, Holy Week is celebrated with much pageantry. Long processions take place from one end of town to the other throughout the days leading up to Easter.

Look at images online of *Semana Santa* (Holy Week) in Guatemala, *alfombras* (carpets made of flowers), and the processions. Study the artwork "Guatemala: Procession" and ponder its depiction of Holy Week in this one Latin American country. Holy Week is an important time in our Christian faith, and processions have been a part of our tradition since the very first one in which Jesus entered Jerusalem.

Supplies:

- Bibles (Matthew 21:1–90, Mark 11:1–10, Luke 19:28–38)
- artwork: "Guatemala: Procession" by Betty LaDuke, found on Google Images
- computer with Internet access, preferably with projection capability
- pictures of *Semana Santa* in Guatemala, *alfombras*, and processions, found on Google Images

Option 1:

- glass jars for each person
- multiple colors of sand (available at any craft store)
- craft sticks

Option 2:

- 8" x 10" card stock or larger for each person
- glue
- multiple colors of sand
- pencils

Talk with the children about Palm Sunday and Holy Week. Ask them to tell you what they know about how they're celebrated in your congregation. Show them where in the Bible they can read about the beginning of these Christian traditions. Display the artwork "Guatemala: Procession." Ask them what they see in the picture. What do they think of all the colors? Who do they see? What images stand out for them? If you're able, show them the pictures from Google Images (on supplies list).

Many people in Latin America live in poverty, and the church has become a place of rest and relief for them. They make a weeklong celebration of Holy Week that doesn't only take place in the church during worship, but involves the entire community. This week reminds them that God loves them and wants them to have lives filled with joy and hope. The elaborate colors and processions help them experience beauty as connected to the very heart of their faith. Life in Guatemala is filled with color. Their clothing is colorful, the landscape is colorful, and everywhere you look there's an abundance of color.

Option 1: Have the children make colorful sand sculptures in jars. Each person layers the different colors in the jar provided. Use craft sticks to push the sand around in the jar to make a design.

Option 2: Have the children draw a picture. Spread the glue within the lines and pour the sand over the glue. These pictures will need to dry before they can be taken home. Have the children talk about their designs.

FLY A KITE

Leader preparation: Kites are often used in celebrations to express the winds of the Spirit or prayers sent heavenward. Kites are used in Guatemala for the Day of the Dead celebration, which is an observance of All Saints' Day; in Greece at the beginning of Lent; and in Bermuda on Good Friday. Watch the YouTube video "Bermuda—Good Friday Celebration." Read about the tradition of "Clean Monday" and "Bermuda Kites" on Wikipedia. Decide if you'll show these videos to the children or what information you'll share. Make a sample kite using one of these websites: "Wikihow—Kite" or "Big Wind Kites."

Supplies:

- (optional) computer with Internet access
- (optional) digital projector
- (optional) video: "Bermuda—Good Friday Celebration," found on YouTube
- supplies and directions for making a kite from websites "Wikihow—Kite" or "Big Wind Kites"
- sample kite

Tell the children that kites are used in many countries on holy days. Flying a kite can be part of the celebration rituals for Pentecost, Clean Monday (first Monday in Lent) in Greece, Good Friday/Easter in Bermuda, and Day of the Dead (All Saints' Day) in Guatemala. Show one or both videos, if you choose, and share information you have learned about the kite traditions in the different countries.

Suggest that when they feel the wind tugging on a kite, it's easy to imagine that it's the breath of God blowing on the kite. A high-soaring kite can help them visualize prayers going out to God or the spirits of those who have died going to heaven. Show the children the kite you made. Invite the children to make their own kites following your directions. After the kites are made, try flying them outside, if possible, and invite the children to say a prayer while flying their kites.

ACTIVITIES FOR
YOUNGER
CHILDREN
(AGES 3-6)

The fun activities in this chapter will encourage this
eager age group to develop their faith life as they pray,
play, and learn about Lent and Easter.

THE CHURCH YEAR AND CELEBRATION STATIONS: LENT AND EASTER

Leader preparation: The church year provides many opportunities for celebrations and traditions. Young children love celebrations and enjoy marking traditions with activities. Consider the various Lent and Easter traditions in your church and how they're celebrated. Review "The Church Year" document and "Celebration Stations: Lent and Easter" explanation and activities. Gather supplies and set up the stations. Decide how you want the children to explore the stations, such as rotating in intervals or wandering as they choose.

Supplies:
- "The Church Year," page 49
- supplies for stations
- (optional) adult helpers

Ask the children which seasonal holidays they enjoy. Tell them the church has seasons and special days, too. Use the talking points on the "The Church Year" to explain the church year to the children, emphasizing Lent and Easter. Introduce the celebration stations and invite them to explore them as you've determined.

THE CHURCH YEAR

The church has a calendar that revolves around the life of Jesus. Although the activities in this chapter focus on Lent and Easter, an overview of the entire church calendar is given here.

The church calendar begins with the four weeks of **Advent**, which is the time before Christmas when people in the church prepare for the birth of Jesus on Christmas day.

The church calendar continues with the season of **Christmas** to the day of **Epiphany**, January 6, when we celebrate the visit of the wise men.

The church year has two times called **Ordinary Time**, which aren't ordinary at all, but rather, counts the Sundays until the next season. The first Ordinary Time is from Epiphany to the season of Lent. During Ordinary Time we learn about Jesus and his life and teachings.

Lent is a time for prayer and penitence. Penitence is a big word that means, "I'm sorry, God." Lent is the 40 days leading up to Holy Week and Easter.

Holy Week begins with **Palm Sunday**, when Jesus rode into Jerusalem on a donkey and many people greeted him as a king. In the days following, Jesus had his last supper with his disciples, was betrayed by one of them, taken to the courts, was crucified, and died on the cross.

On **Easter** day we celebrate that God raised Jesus from the dead, that he is alive, and that he visited with many of his friends. During the season of Easter we celebrate the resurrection of Jesus and that he sent the Holy Spirit to be with us always.

Pentecost is called "the birthday of the church" because that's the day the Holy Spirit came upon the disciples and many others in Jerusalem. Jesus' disciples started to preach and teach, and others wanted to be followers of Jesus. This was how the church began long, long ago.

After Pentecost is another season of Ordinary Time, counting the Sundays until we are back to Advent.

CELEBRATION STATIONS: SPOTLIGHT ON LENT AND EASTER

Set up stations in your space for Lent and Easter. Each station offers two activities. Use one or both, or substitute with an activity of your own choosing that has special significance to your church or community. Add décor and symbols at each station to enhance the theme. Suggestions are given, but use your own creativity and available supplies as well. You will need an adult helper at each station to guide the children as they explore that station.

LENT CELEBRATION STATION

Display suggestions: Ashes, crosses, nails, palm branches, liturgical color of purple, a Lenten cross, pretzels, banners appropriate for Lent

PRETZEL FORGIVENESS PRAYER

Provide each child with a full-size pretzel. Tell them they'll use the pretzel to help them with prayers of forgiveness. Read the following examples of things for which the children might want to ask forgiveness. Tell them when they hear something for which they would like to ask forgiveness they can say that thing to themselves in their heart and take a bite of the pretzel.

Bite 1: Ask forgiveness in a family relationship.

Bite 2: Ask forgiveness in a friendship.

Bite 3: Ask forgiveness in matters of cruelness or thoughtlessness toward creatures or creation.

Bite 4: Ask forgiveness for those with whom you have quarreled or fought.

Bite 5: Ask God to remind you that God forgives us in all things.

End the prayer with: *Thanks be to God. Amen!*

PALM SUNDAY PLAY

Invite the children to act out Palm Sunday. Use pieces of green crepe-paper streamers, ribbons, or pieces of material for palm branches. Let someone pretend to be the donkey that Jesus rode upon. Shout "Hosanna" and sing a Palm Sunday song, if desired.

EASTER CELEBRATION STATION

Display suggestions: An empty cross, an empty tomb, flowers—especially lilies—plastic eggs (opened up to look like an empty tomb), butterflies, banners appropriate for Easter (white: the liturgical color)

HIDE-AND-SEEK

Tell the children that when Jesus was in the tomb, he was hidden from his followers. When they went to seek Jesus on Easter morning, he was GONE! Play a game of hide-and-seek in honor of that mystery.

BUTTERFLY CRAFT

The Easter/Resurrection message is like caterpillars going into cocoons and becoming butterflies. Make simple butterflies by placing colorful tissue paper into the clip part of a clothespin and fluffing out the tissue paper. Use a twist tie to secure it and also to serve as the antenna. Ask the person in charge of your worship space if they can be displayed in the sanctuary for your Easter Sunday worship service.

ACTIVITIES FOR
INTERGENERATIONAL
GROUPS

The following Lent and Easter activities will celebrate
and accommodate the broad spectrum of faith
development and life experiences in this all-ages group.

HOLY LINENS

Leader preparation: Paraments are the cloths that cover the pulpit, Bible, and communion table or altar. Make sure that either the sanctuary or storage area where paraments or banners are kept is available for the group to explore.

Centering Prayer: *Artful Weaver, help me feel your delight at all of the brightly colored threads that pattern your world. Help me trust in your vision for beautiful designs that are unfolding. Where threads have broken, guide all your people toward healing practices that honor the hurt places and that open our eyes to new beauty that may emerge from them. Amen.*

Supplies:

- Bible
- (optional) someone in your church who helps care for the paraments and can answer the group's questions
- (optional) a collection of yarn including the colors blue, purple, and red

Ask the group to listen closely to the scripture reading, paying special attention to what both men and women brought and what the women donated on their own. Read Exodus 35:20–29. If available, spread out a variety of yarn, and have the children pick out the colors of yarn the women spun. Talk about how these colors are used in your own church in different seasons of the church year, such as Advent, Lent, Easter, and Pentecost. Typically, blue and purple are the "getting ready" colors used during Lent and Advent in anticipation of Easter and Christmas. White symbolizes the new life of Jesus' resurrection. Red symbolizes the fire of the Holy Spirit during Pentecost. Green symbolizes the Ordinary Time of daily ministry.

EGG HUNT

Leader preparation: This is a good activity to do close to Easter. Plan a space where children and youth can dye eggs and find a place to hide them for an egg hunt. Recruit additional adults to help dye and hide the eggs.

Supplies:
- hard-boiled eggs
- egg dye
- coverings for work spaces
- aprons or old shirts for each member of the group
- children's story Bible

Invite the group to dye eggs. As the eggs dry and someone has gone to hide them, gather the group to hear the story of the death of Moses. From a children's story Bible, read Deuteronomy 34:1–12. Invite comments and questions about the story. When Moses died, the people were sad. Even the people who had argued with Moses when he was alive were sad. Around Easter time, we hear the story about how Jesus died.

Discuss:
- How did people react when Jesus died?
- How did people react when God raised Jesus from the dead?

The good news we celebrate at Easter is that Jesus was raised from the dead. Just as God raised Jesus from the dead, so God raises us from death, too. How might the eggs we dyed remind us of the new life Jesus gives us?

Have the group go on an egg hunt to find the eggs they dyed.

BEAUTY HELPS US WORSHIP

Leader preparation: In order to get ready for the elaborate parades of Christian pilgrims through the streets during Holy Week, people in Guatemala create elaborate floral designs, or carpets called *alfombras*, on the streets. As pilgrims walk through the flowers, the designs disappear as faithful feet scatter them. Imagine what it would be like to walk over beautiful *alfombras* in celebration of Holy Week. How do these temporary expressions of beauty that instantly get swept away affect your understanding of beauty? Reflect on the desire to preserve beauty versus the experience of beauty in a moment. Become familiar with the artwork "Guatemala Procession" and the link to Guatemalan *alfombras* found in the supply list so that you can lead your group in appreciating the beauty in both.

Supplies:
- artwork: "Guatemala: Procession" by Betty LaDuke, found on Google Images
- computer with Internet access
- website: www.travelyucatan.com: "Mayan Holy Week Carpets"

Share the artwork "Guatemala: Procession" by Betty LaDuke with your group. LaDuke's paintings are inspired by her travels throughout the world, where she has seen many different ways to worship God using beautiful designs and objects. In her description of this painting, LaDuke says the faces represent masks used in Holy Week processions in the Mayan village of Chichicastenango in Guatemala. If this painting is based on the stories of Holy Week, wonder together who is riding the donkey into the city. Why does the group think the artist chose the colors, animals, and people they see in this painting? Ask the group to name acts of worship they notice. Which acts look familiar? Discuss special ways that your church celebrates Palm Sunday. How does your church use beautiful objects in worship to tell the story of Jesus entering Jerusalem at the beginning of Holy Week?

One way the Mayan people of Guatemala re-tell the story of Holy Week is by creating *alfombras*, or carpets, that line the streets before worshipers walk over them in elaborate processions. These carpets help people remember how Jesus entered Jerusalem. Gather around a computer and view the link listed in the supply list about *alfombras* created during Holy Week in Guatemala. Discover what kinds of materials people use to make *alfombras*. Absorb the beauty of the many different types of carpets created. Note what happens to the carpets when the large Holy Week processions walk through the streets. Under "History," read about the biblical origins of this tradition.

ACTIVITIES FOR
SEEKERS AND THOSE
NEW TO CHURCH

These activities have been designed to welcome adults
and youth with little or no experience in a faith
community to learn about and embrace some of the
church's significant Lent and Easter practices.

THE OTHER CALENDAR SPOTLIGHT ON LENT

Leader preparation: Seekers and those new to church may not know anything about the liturgical seasons of the church year; however, it's possible that, aside from Christmas and Easter, many in the pews don't either. This activity can be shared as an open session during Lent that includes longstanding members of the church who wish to know more about when we celebrate, meditate, remember, and tell the stories of our faith. Opening the group session to everyone who's interested will not only increase the knowledge base of the community, but also has the potential to begin friendships and establish common ground.

As we move through the liturgical season of Lent, invite comments from the group about their own practices during this season. Create a conversation instead of giving a lecture. Invite stories that help make the season meaningful to the group.

Supplies:
- calendar for the current year
- "The Other Calendar: Spotlight on Lent," page 61
- (optional) calendar marking the current liturgical season

Begin by asking people to say words they think of when they hear the word "calendar." We depend on and often appreciate calendars; sometimes we resent their restrictions and reminders of our busy-ness. Most people carry a calendar with them on their cellphone or other electronic device, or have a hard copy in their purse or wallet.

The Christian church also uses a calendar, but it doesn't hang on a wall in the kitchen. It, too, keeps track of birthdays and anniversaries; it reminds us of the holy moments and opportunities to participate and grow in faith. Sometimes we're surprised by what's coming up next when our lives are busy and we're focused on our secular calendar. The liturgical calendar helps us remember our story of faith and worship. Using this calendar of faith, we can tell the story to others and remain faithful in our own lives. By understanding the seasons of the church year, including Lent, which is the focus of this activity, we can live both today and in the grand scope of history and future. Distribute handout. Walk the group through the season of Lent. Invite people to share what they find beautiful about this church season.

THE OTHER CALENDAR
SPOTLIGHT ON LENT

The season of Lent is the 40 days—not counting Sundays—that lead up to Easter. During this time, Christians examine their own lives in light of God's love and the ministry of Jesus. The liturgical color is black or purple—the colors of penitence and mourning. Many churches offer special study or prayer opportunities during Lent, following the example of the Gospels, in which a major portion of Jesus' teaching and healing takes place in the period before he leaves Galilee to go to Jerusalem.

- Is the season of Lent an important educational or spiritual time for your community?

- What might you do during Lent to tell its story?

The last week of Lent begins with Palm/Passion Sunday, a period in which we walk with Jesus during his final week on Earth: his triumphal entry into Jerusalem; his preaching and teaching, especially in the Temple; his last supper with his followers; and his arrest, trial, and crucifixion. Palm branches are often given to the congregation on Palm/Passion Sunday, as the story is told throughout worship, from the joyful entry to the quieter, darker days of the Passion. Palm/Passion colors are purple or red.

- How does your church recognize Palm/Passion Sunday? If the group has attended other churches, they might be able to share stories and memories from those Palm/Passion celebrations that were significant to them.

DELIGHTING THE EYE
LENT AND EASTER

Leader preparation: Color is one way we tell our story to ourselves. Check with your worship leaders or minister to see in what ways your congregation deliberately uses color during Lent and Easter. Ask if the group can look through the storage closet that contains the paraments, stoles, and banners. If you have time, take a look before the session begins, so you can tailor your conversation to this particular faith community. If the minister has stoles for Lent and Easter, ask to borrow them or invite him or her to come to the session to talk about them.

Supplies:
- paraments used within the church community (You may wish to leave them in storage and take the group to see them if possible.)
- stoles from the minister's collection, if available
- fabric or paint color swatches, if paraments and stoles aren't available
- paper
- (optional) colored pencils or markers

The story of faith is told in song, story, and color. Each season of the year uses a color that helps tell its story. The sanctuary is adorned with these colors to help the congregation find beauty, understand the story, and remember the season we are experiencing. For much of the history of Christianity, only a small minority of the faithful were able to read. If the community had a Bible—and many did not—it was not written in the language of the people, but rather in Latin, Greek, or Hebrew. The history of the church, the names and adventures of the faithful of other generations, and the ancient tales of the Old and New Testaments were told in story, mosaic, or stained glass (when there were buildings constructed deliberately as sanctuaries); or in the banners, stoles, and paraments of the season. We continue the tradition of visual narrative today. There are no strict rules about what colors to use. Indeed, traditions around the use of color have changed over the centuries.

The most common liturgical colors used during Lent and Easter are red, white, and violet (or purple).

• **Red** symbolizes blood, life, and the Holy Spirit. Traditionally, red is used for Palm/Passion Sunday, Pentecost, and other days when we're focusing on the movement of the Holy Spirit among us.

• **White** indicates purity, and is displayed for Easter and Christmas, as well as for weddings, funerals, and memorial services. **Gold** is a variant of white, symbolizing the richness of the faithful life.

• **Violet, purple, and black** are the colors of repentance and mourning, and are used for Lent and Advent. Sometimes these colors are also used for funerals or memorial services.

Invite the group to look at the ways your church uses color during Lent and Easter. As you move around the sanctuary, take note of the colors in the room: floor, walls, windows, communion table or altar, pews, choir chairs, worship leaders' chairs. Celebrate the gifts of color, texture, and shape in telling the story of faith. Tour the sanctuary to see which colors are teaching the community now. Which colors are permanent (floor and wall coverings, furniture), and which change with the liturgical seasons? Return to your meeting room. Talk about the liturgical seasons with which you are most familiar. What are your favorites? Why?

Option: If your faith community does not use banners and paraments or does not have a sanctuary, use paper and colored pencils or markers to create some suggested visual lessons for Lent and Easter.

SHARING FOOD

Leader preparation: Many of the stories about Jesus involved gathering around food. Jesus lifted up bread and wine during the Passover feast as a remembrance of him and a blessing for all of us. Call to mind some Gospel stories of the tables where Jesus shared food. Search Google Images for a picture of Jesus smiling or laughing. In the spirit of hospitality toward seekers and those new to church, set a welcome table for them in your fellowship hall or social room, away from the meeting space, if possible. This is intended to be a snack, not a meal, and a time for mingling and visiting with one another as the start of building community.

Supplies:
- Bibles
- fish-shaped crackers
- small variety of breads
- (optional) spreads to put on breads
- small variety of fruit or cheese
- an image of Jesus smiling or laughing, found on Google Images

Invite everyone into the circle of chairs. Pass out the Bibles. Introduce the story by saying that it's an Easter story, an event that occurred after Jesus' crucifixion. Have the group members take turns reading John 21:1–20. How do you feel about this story? What questions does it raise?

Ask people to imagine themselves as the disciples. Invite them to close their eyes, if they wish, and to imagine losing a very close, dear friend to the horrible death of crucifixion, remembering their own cowardice on the night their friend was arrested. You are overcome with grief and fearing the authorities, as it's well known that you were his disciple. And now you see that very dear friend appearing before you. What feelings well up in you? What thoughts swirl around in your mind? How do you cope with such intense feelings, such impossible things happening? Jesus' disciples decided to go fishing. Pause and invite the learners to open their eyes. Ask them to take a deep breath. Then invite everyone to the table you've prepared.

SERVING ONE ANOTHER

Leader preparation: In many congregations, foot washing is a common ritual practiced during Holy Week. This activity offers your group an opportunity to experiment with the ministry of foot washing within its own borders, to discuss why or why not it is important, or uncomfortable, or meaningful. Don't expect people to accept new (or old) ideas immediately, but rather, offer different ways in which practices can be tried. Offer this activity as an experiment in trying new things, or in reconsidering what may have lost some meaning through repetition.

Let your group know about this ritual ahead of time so they're prepared to remove their socks and shoes without too much difficulty. Suggest that everyone brings their own towel. Invite people to think about the ways we serve others by washing their feet, and the ways we receive care by allowing our own feet to be washed.

Arrange your space with chairs set in a circle with enough room to allow for movement between and in front of each place. Put a basin and pitcher of warm water by each chair.

Supplies:
- Bibles: John 13:1–17, 31b–35, and Acts 2:42–47
- basins for washing
- pitchers of warm water
- towels
- (optional) sanitary hand wipes

Do this activity in silence once the foot washing has begun. Explain what's going to happen and invite people to place their bare feet in the basin in front of them. Read the Bible passages. Pause for a few moments of silence and meditation. Offer a prayer asking that God will open their eyes to new ways of understanding what's being practiced in this place. Move to the first person, kneel at the basin, and pour the water over the person's feet. Rinse the feet, then dry them with the towel. Return to your seat. The one whose feet are now clean moves to the next person and repeats the process. The last person will wash the feet of the leader. Then sit in meditative silence for a few moments.

An alternative to foot washing is using sanitary hand wipes and disposing of the wipes after use. These wipes are usually cool to the touch, and the evaporating alcohol will make feet cool, so you might also want to use some towels.

Afterward, or at your next session, invite conversation about the experience of washing and being washed. What insights did the imitation of the Gospel text open? If foot washing is a common practice in your community, ask what meaning it has for those who participate. If this is a new experience, was it helpful in understanding discipleship, or in becoming more comfortable with the idea of foot washing in the community? In Jesus' time, the host washed the feet of the guests who entered his or her home. How do we care for one another and offer hospitality? How might we expand our current practice of hospitality, moving beyond our own comfort level and into extravagant offerings of grace?

WORSHIP RESOURCES FOR LENT, HOLY WEEK, AND EASTER

These special worship elements infuse scripture, sacred tradition, and creativity into a truly meaningful Lent and Easter experience for your entire congregation.

CHILDREN'S MESSAGE
ENGAGING THE WORD
RESPONDING TO THE WORD
"ASHES AND WISHES"

Leader preparation: Name something about yourself you would like to change in order to be a better steward of God's gifts. Reflect on it as you gather supplies for this activity that connects well with Ash Wednesday or the first Sunday in Lent.

Supplies:
- small pieces of paper
- pens or pencils
- a can and a match

Begin by sharing about the season of Lent as a time of change. Invite worshipers to think of something about their lives that they would like to change in order to become better stewards of God's gifts, that is, better disciples of Jesus. Allow time to write these on the slips of paper. Invite ushers (maybe children) to collect the slips in a can. In some Ash Wednesday services, this might be considered the offering. Say a prayer of blessing once the can, full of hopes and wishes for change, is returned to you. Ask someone to take the can outside and burn the slips, so that you now have a burnt offering before God.

Later in worship, invite worshipers to come forward one by one for the imposition of ashes. Rub some of the ashes from the burned slips between your thumb and forefinger and make the sign of the cross on each person's forehead (or on the back of one hand) as they come forward. As you impose the ashes, say, "[Name], remember that you are dust and to dust you shall return. Turn away from your sins and believe in God's good news." Close with a prayer asking God to help us change, so that we might become faithful disciples and stewards.

A WORSHIP CUSTOM FROM THE EARLY CHURCH: BRINGING STORIES AND FOOD TO SHARE

Prepare to enter this experience. The season of Lent begins with Ash Wednesday and extends until Easter Vigil and Easter Sunday. It's a time to focus on the life of Jesus and our lives as disciples, exploring the ways we give and receive hospitality. When Jesus washed the disciples' feet, he showed them that they needed to be able to receive hospitality. Good disciples need to keep giving and sharing hospitality.

Lent is also a season of telling the stories of salvation. From the days of the earliest church, Lent focused on mentoring those who would become Christians through baptism at the Easter vigil. How do we relate these two themes? Quite simply. At the same time we as Christians go about our lives as disciples living out lives rooted in hospitality, we take the time of Lent as an opportunity to review our theology, beliefs, and the covenants we have made with God. We affirm them, and at the same time focus on our roles as teachers and mentors for those who are eager to learn the faith. A tall order? Perhaps, but not a dual role. Some of our best teaching is done by example. What better way to spend Lent than by extending real hospitality and telling stories?

How to use this idea in worship: Food in church? From the earliest Christian worship, people brought their food and shared it. They took turns telling the stories of their faith, singing songs and reciting scripture. Here is something in which everyone can participate—even visitors and newcomers can enjoy the food and listen to the stories without pressure, but can certainly be given an opportunity to share their own stories. Make Lent a time for genuine hospitality. Allow plenty of advance time to prepare for this activity. Perhaps a small planning group could work out details of the following and do adequate publicity. Choose a time during worship for the story and snack time. Plan to have this happen every Sunday at the same point in the service. Recruit families, representatives of a church committee, or individuals to commit to a Sunday. Make sure they know their expectations before they commit.

The task:

a) Prepare to present a story of faith. It can be a Bible story, a story of Christian faith and belief, a life experience that was important to their faith journey, or a story about baptism. Set a time limit of no more than 5 or 10 minutes. The group can bring pictures, props, or a PowerPoint.

b) Recommend a hymn that relates to their story. Let the musicians know in advance so they can provide accompaniment.

c) Prepare a short prayer. Consider printing it in the order of service for all to pray.

d) Bring some food to share that's easy to handle. Ask planners to assist in the preparation.

At an appointed time in the service, have the worship leader say something like: "During our services on the Sundays of Lent, we will include a custom from the early Christian church. It's a time of hospitality and sharing of food. Just like in the early church where the members brought their life experiences, stories of salvation and baptism, and songs, we've recruited members of our congregation who are willing to do that for our worship. During a time of some instrumental music (a brief song) we will have something to eat and then we will hear their stories."

Adapt this to what works in your setting. Open up the storytelling for others to add their faith stories, and as a great example of genuine hospitality, invite visitors to tell theirs. In addition, a time of fellowship following the service of worship would be a great time to hear more stories. This is a way for Lent to be a time of deepening faith and hospitality for everyone.

A RITE OF PENANCE AND RECONCILIATION FOR LENT

Leader preparation: Consider offering the following rite to your community's acts or prayers of confession as a Lenten preparation for the coming of Holy Week. Distribute magician's flash paper and pencils. Invite your congregation to write a word or a prayer for forgiveness for something in their own lives, their community, or their nation.

Supplies:
- magician's flash paper for each person
- pencils
- candle
- matches

Flash paper creates no ash and burns quickly when ignited. Demonstrate the burning of flash paper with a candle and say, "Through the light of Christ, we seek and find forgiveness and reconciliation." Invite the group to come forward and burn the paper themselves, or hand the paper to the leader to burn. The group may say a prayer as it's burned or simply say the words "forgiveness" or "reconciliation."

Conclude with the following prayer: *Loving God, you call us, your children, to be agents of your grace, but we so often disappoint. As we are given assurance of forgiveness, we ask for the fire of your Holy Spirit to pour out upon us all to do the hard work of reconciliation in our homes, our communities, and our nation. We are an imperfect people who deserve your judgment, but we hope to move into a new holiness that helps us to pray more honestly the words "Thy kingdom come, thy will be done on earth as it is in heaven." Amen.*

DRAMATIC READING OF SCRIPTURE: THE PASSION

This is a worship experience that invites people of all ages and abilities in your congregation to participate in the Passion story. Although it appears complicated, it's actually a reading of the scripture in dramatic format. It follows the text closely and allows the congregation to portray the story of Jesus' experiences of betrayal, denial, and isolation. It can be divided to take place over two Sundays; or each of the elements can stand alone and be used as part of a worship service.

GATHERING: TRAIL OF SORROW

Leader preparation: Select a cast of actors to dress in classical biblical clothing. Rehearse the song, "Were You There?" (found in most hymnals). Gather props to represent Christ's passion.

Supplies:
- large cross
- large Bible
- large stone (theatrical stone made of paper and painted)
- classical biblical clothing (homemade costumes)

As a processional into the sanctuary, use a dramatic pageantry of characters from the Passion. Have them march in carrying props from the story. Include in the march: Roman soldiers, disciples, the women, high priests, Pilate, and Jesus. Project the lyrics of the song along with depictions of the Passion while the choir and congregation sing "Were You There?"

OPENING PRAYER: SPEAKING TO GOD

Leader preparation: Become familiar with the prayer "Speaking to God." Make copies of the prayer, or prepare it for projection.

Supplies:

• copies of "Speaking to God" prayer, below, or computer and projector

Invite the congregation to pray the prayer in unison.

SPEAKING TO GOD

O God, merciful and loving Creator, your people have gathered, and we stand before you with all our faults and frailties. We come into your house of prayer because we honor and worship you. We bring our joys and pains, our burdens and concerns. Here we are, O God, just as we are, with our lives in your hands.

In the beauty of this day, we listen to hear your still-speaking voice. The chirping of birds, the scurrying of critters, the crying of infants, and the shining brilliance of the sun all remind us of your constant presence with us. Your love touches us and lifts our souls.

In this moment, God, give us courage in the struggle for justice and peace. Fill us with your Holy Spirit. Come now, Caring Just One, for you are our God, and we are your people. We pray that we will find favor in your sight as we seek to do your will.

Hallelujah! Shalom. Salaam. Right on! Amen.

RESPONSIVE READING
PSALM 119:105–112, 129–136

Leader preparation: Make copies of the responsive reading based on Psalm 119, or prepare it for projection. Recruit a leader for the reading.

Supplies:

- copies of *Responsive Reading: Psalm 119:105–112, 129–136* on page 77 or computer and projector

Use the responsive reading of Psalm 119:105–112, 129–136.

PSALM 119:105–112, 129–136

Leader: Your word is a lamp to my feet and a light to my path.

People: I have sworn an oath and confirmed it, to observe your righteous ordinances.

Leader: I am severely afflicted; give me life, O God, according to your word.

People: Accept my offerings of praise, O God, and teach me your ordinances.

Leader: I hold my life in my hand continually, but I do not forget your law.

People: The wicked have laid a snare for me, but I do not stray from your precepts.

Leader: Your decrees are my heritage forever; they are the joy of my heart.

People: Incline my heart to perform your statutes forever, to the end.

Leader: Your decrees are wonderful; therefore my soul keeps them.

People: The unfolding of your words gives light; it imparts understanding to the simple.

Leader: With open mouth I pant, because I long for your commandments.

People: Turn to me and be gracious to me, as is your custom toward those who love your name.

Leader: Keep my steps steady according to your promise, and never let iniquity have dominion over me.

People: Redeem me from human oppression, that I may keep your precepts.

Leader: Make your face shine upon your servant, and teach me your statutes.

People: My eyes shed streams of tears because your law is not kept.

PAIN AND SUFFERING BEFORE JOY
DRAMATIZATION OF MATTHEW 26:14–75

Leader preparation: Read Matthew 26:14–75. As you study the play based on this reading, determine who will be the actors. Recruit people to design the sets and conduct rehearsals. This requires considerable time for creativity and imagination. Create a support team of artists, technicians, and laborers. Involve the entire congregation.

Supplies:

- copies of "Pain and Suffering before Joy: Dramatization Based on Matthew 26:14–75" on pages 79–82
- classical biblical period clothing
- props for set design
- table
- bread and grape juice
- cast of actors
- stage crew
- sound effects
- lighting grid
- audio board with microphones
- swords, clubs
- designated space in congregation

PAIN AND SUFFERING BEFORE JOY
DRAMATIZATION OF MATTHEW 26:14–75

Cast: Narrator, Judas, Peter, Jesus, First man, Second man, Caiaphas, Religious leader, First girl, Second girl, Woman

SCENE 1

Narrator: One of Jesus' twelve disciples, who was called Judas Iscariot, went to the chief priest and religious leaders and said:

Judas: What will you give me if I betray him to you?

Narrator: The religious leaders paid Judas thirty pieces of silver. And from that moment he began to look for an opportunity to betray the Messiah. On the first day of Passover when unleavened bread was prepared and eaten, Jesus' disciples came to him and said:

Peter: Where do you want us to make the preparations for you to eat the Passover?

Jesus: Go into the city to a certain man, and say to him, "The Teacher says, 'My time is near; I will keep the Passover at your house with my disciples.'"

Narrator: So the disciples did as Jesus had directed them, and they prepared the Passover meal. That night, Jesus took his place with the twelve; and while they were eating, he said:

Jesus: Truly I tell you, one of you will betray me.

Peter: *(He is agitated, along with the other disciples who are greatly distressed.)* Surely not I, Lord?

Jesus: The one who has dipped his hand into the bowl with me will betray me. The Human One goes as it is written of him, but woe to that one by whom the Human One is betrayed! It would have been better for that one not to have been born.

Judas: Surely not I, Rabbi?

Jesus: You have said so. *(Jesus takes a loaf of bread, blesses it, breaks it, and gives it to his disciples.)* Take, eat; this is my body. *(Jesus takes a cup, gives thanks, and hands it to his disciples.)* Drink from it, all of you, for this is my blood of the covenant, which is poured out for many for the forgiveness of sins. I tell you, I will never again drink of this fruit of the vine until that day when I drink it new with you in God's kingdom.

(The disciples begin to sing a hymn and start to walk out.)

Jesus: You will all become deserters because of me this night; for it is written, "I will strike the shepherd, and the sheep of the flock will be scattered." But after I am raised up, I will go ahead of you to Galilee.

Peter: Though all become deserters because of you, I will never desert you.

Jesus: Truly I tell you, this very night, before the cock crows, you will deny me three times.

Peter: Even though I must die with you, I will not deny you. *(Disciples nod and murmur in agreement with Peter. Jesus leads the disciples across stage to a garden and stops by a tree.)*

SCENE 2

Narrator: Jesus went with the disciples to a place called Gethsemane and said to them:

Jesus: Sit here while I go over there and pray. *(Peter and the two disciples walk with Jesus away from the other disciples. Jesus is agitated and turns to Peter.)* I am deeply grieved, even to death; remain here, and stay awake with me.

(Jesus goes away and throws himself on the ground and prays.) Abba, if it is possible, let this cup pass from me; yet not what I want, but what you want.

(Jesus walks to his disciples, who are asleep, and shakes Peter.) So, could you not stay awake with me one hour? Stay awake and pray that you may not come into the time of trial; the spirit indeed is willing, but the flesh is weak.

(Jesus walks away again; stops and prays. He is in agony.) Abba, if this cannot pass unless I drink it, your will be done.

(Jesus walks back to Peter and the other two and finds them sleeping. He turns away from them and takes a few steps. He stops, falls on his knees, weeps, and prays again.)

Abba, if this cannot pass unless I drink it, your will be done.

(Jesus stands up and returns to Peter and the others.)

Are you still sleeping and taking your rest? See, the hour is at hand, and the Human One is betrayed into the hands of sinners. Get up, let us be going. See, my betrayer is at hand.

SCENE 3

(Judas comes with the chief priests and religious leaders. Some are carrying swords and clubs. Judas walks up to Jesus and kisses him on the face.)

Judas: Greetings, Rabbi!

Man: *(carrying a sword)* You are under arrest!

Jesus: *(turns to Judas)* Friend, do what you are here to do.

(The man with the sword grabs Jesus by the arm and leads Jesus away. Peter pulls his sword and swings at the other man, who has Jesus' arm.)

Jesus: Put your sword back into its place; for all who take the sword will perish by the sword. Do you think that I cannot appeal to God, who will at once send me more than twelve legions of angels? But how then would the scriptures be fulfilled, which say it must happen in this way? Have you come out with swords and clubs to arrest me as though I were a bandit? Day after day I sat in the temple teaching, and you did not arrest me. But all this has taken place, so that the scriptures of the prophets may be fulfilled. *(Everyone leaves the stage.)*

SCENE 4

Narrator: The disciples all deserted Jesus. Those who had arrested him went to the home of Caiaphas, the high priest, where the scribes and the elders had gathered. Peter followed at a distance, as far as the courtyard of the high priest; and going inside, he sat with the guards in order to see how this would end. Now the chief priests and the whole council were looking for false testimony against Jesus so that they might put him to death, but they found none, though many false witnesses came forward. At last two came forward. *(Two men stand up from the audience and point toward Jesus at the side of stage.)*

First man: This fellow said, "I am able to destroy the temple of God and build it in three days."

Second man: He said he could build the great temple in three days.

Caiaphas: *(stands up)* Have you no answer? What is it that they testify against you? *(Jesus silently stares at the two men.)*

Caiaphas: I put you under oath before the living God. Tell us if you are the Messiah, the Son of God.

Jesus: You have said so. But I tell you, from now on you will see the Human One seated at the right hand of Power and coming on the clouds of heaven.

Caiaphas: *(tears his clothes)* He has blasphemed! Why do we still need witnesses? You have now heard his blasphemy. What is your verdict?

Religious leader: He deserves death.

(The crowd jeers. A man slaps Jesus on his face.)

First man: Prophesy to us, you Messiah!

Second man: Who is it that struck you?

(The crowd laughs along with the religious leaders.)

SCENE 5

Narrator: Peter was sitting outside in the courtyard near a young servant girl.

Girl: You also were with Jesus the Galilean.

Peter: *(Stands up and walks to middle of stage toward a second girl.)* No, I wasn't. I do not know what you are talking about.

Second girl: This man was with Jesus of Nazareth.

Peter: You are a liar! I do not know the man.

(The crowd walks up to Peter.)

Woman: Certainly you are also one of them, for your accent betrays you.

Peter: I swear to God, I do not know the man!

(The sound of a rooster crows.)

Peter: *(Weeps bitterly and speaks, mostly to himself.)* Jesus said before the cock crows, I will have denied him three times. *(He cries uncontrollably.)*

Sing a congregational hymn of your choice.

HOPE BRINGS JOY
DRAMATIZATION OF MATTHEW 27

Leader preparation: Read Matthew 27. Study the play based on the reading, audition actors, design sets, and conduct rehearsals. This requires considerable time for creativity and imagination; to recruit support teams of artists, technicians, and laborers; and to get the congregation involved in the scripture story.

Supplies:

- copies of "Hope Brings Joy: Dramatization of Matthew 27," pages 85–88
- biblical period clothing
- props for set design
- pieces of silver
- cast of actors
- stage crew
- sound effects
- lighting grid
- audio board with microphones
- designated space in the congregation

HOPE BRINGS JOY
DRAMATIZATION OF MATTHEW 27

Cast: Narrator, Judas, Caiaphas, Pilate, Jesus, First soldier, Second soldier, Woman, Man, Joseph

SCENE 1

Narrator: Peter cried all night after the cock crowed three times. He denied Jesus, and the other disciples deserted Jesus. Jesus faced his accusers all alone. Early the next morning, the religious leaders called together the elders of the people. They conferred against Jesus in order to bring about his death. They bound him, led him away, and handed him over to Pilate the governor. When Judas, his betrayer, saw that Jesus was condemned, he repented and brought back the thirty pieces of silver to the chief priests and the elders.

Judas: I have sinned by betraying innocent blood.

Caiaphas: What is that to us? See to it yourself.

Judas: Take back your money. I don't want it. *(Judas screams in agony, throws down the pieces of silver and runs away.)*

Caiaphas: *(Reaches down and picks up the pieces of silver.)* It is not lawful to put these silver pieces into the treasury, since they are blood money. Here, let's buy the potter's field as a place where we can bury foreigners who die in our city.

Narrator: To this very day, that plot of land is still called the Field of Blood. That fulfilled what had been spoken through the prophet Jeremiah who said, "And they took the thirty pieces of silver, the price of the one on whom a price had been set, on whom some of the people of Israel had set a price, and they gave them for the potter's field, as the Lord commanded me." As for Judas, his act of betrayal was too great a burden for him. He ran from the temple and went and hanged himself. Jesus was taken to stand before Pilate, the governor.

SCENE 2

Pilate: Are you the King of the Jews?

Jesus: You say so.

Pilate: Do you not hear how many accusations they make against you? Sedition, incitement, treason, blasphemy.

Narrator: Jesus stared directly at Pilate but gave him no answer, not even to a single charge, so that the governor was greatly amazed. Meanwhile, at the festival the governor was accustomed to release a prisoner for the crowd, anyone whom they wanted. At that time there was a notorious prisoner called

Jesus Barabbas. Pilate realized that it was out of jealousy that the religious leaders and elders of the people had handed Jesus over to him. But Pilate's wife sent word to him, "Have nothing to do with that innocent man, for today I have suffered a great deal because of a dream about him."

Pilate: Whom do you want me to release for you, Jesus Barabbas or Jesus who is called the Messiah?

Caiaphas: *(Turns to the audience.)* People, tell Pilate you want Barabbas! Scream as loud as you can, "We want Barabbas! We want Barabbas! We want Barabbas!" Join me now ... say it, "We want Barabbas! We want Barabbas!"

Pilate: *(Turns to the audience.)* Which of the two do you want me to release for you?

Audience: We want Barabbas! We want Barabbas!

Pilate: Then what should I do with Jesus who is called the Messiah?

Audience: Crucify him! Let him be crucified!

Pilate: Why, what evil has he done?

Caiaphas: *(Turns to Pilate.)* Give us Barabbas. Free Barabbas!

Audience: Give us Barabbas! Give us Barabbas!

Pilate: *(Takes a bowl and fills it with water to wash his hands.)* I am innocent of this man's blood; see to it yourselves.

Audience: His blood be on us and on our children!

Pilate: Go away. I will release Barabbas! You are killing an innocent man.

SCENE 3

Narrator: Jesus, was taken away, beaten, and carried into the governor's headquarters where soldiers stripped him and put a scarlet robe on him, and after twisting some thorns into a crown, they put it on his head. They put a reed in his right hand, knelt before him, and mocked him.

First soldier: Hail, King of the Jews!

Second soldier: Some king you turned out to be!

First soldier: Where is your army, king? *(Pulls off Jesus' clothes and throws an old robe around him.)*

Narrator: They led Jesus away to be crucified. They came upon a man from Cyrene named Simon; they compelled this man to carry his cross. And when they came to a place called Golgotha *(which means "Skull Place")*, they offered Jesus sour wine to drink.

Second soldier: Hey, king, have a drink on us. *(He hands Jesus a cup. Jesus drinks it and spits it out quickly. The soldiers laugh loudly.)*

Narrator: They took Jesus and placed him on a cross and killed him. Over his head they put the charge against him, which read, "This is Jesus, the King of the Jews." Two bandits were crucified with him, one on his right and one on his left. People came by, and as they watched what was happening, they began to deride Jesus.

Woman: You who would destroy the temple and build it in three days, save yourself!

Man: If you are the Son of God, come down from the cross.

Caiaphas: He saved others; he cannot save himself. He is the King of Israel; let him come down from the cross now, and we will believe in him. He trusts in God; let God deliver him now, if God wants to; for he said, "I am God's Son."

Narrator: Even the bandits who were crucified with him also taunted him in the same way. From noon on, darkness came over the whole land until three in the afternoon.

Jesus: *Eli, Eli, lama sabachthani?* My God, my God, why have you forsaken me?

Man: This man is calling for Elijah.

Woman: Give him something to drink. Give him some wine and let him drink.

Caiaphas: Wait, let us see whether Elijah will come to save him.

Jesus: *(Cries with a loud voice.)* My God! My God! *(Jesus dies.)*

Narrator: At that moment the curtain of the temple was torn in two, from top to bottom. The earth shook and the rocks were split. The tombs also were opened, and many bodies of the saints who had fallen asleep were raised. After his resurrection they came out of the tombs and entered the holy city and appeared to many. Now when the centurion and those with him, who were keeping watch over Jesus, saw the earthquake and what took place, they were terrified.

First soldier: Truly this man was God's Son!

Second soldier: *(trembling with fear)* How could this be? What kind of man was he that earth shakes and the dead rise up? Yes, truly, he was the Son of God.

SCENE 4

Narrator: There were many women there who witnessed everything that happened. Looking from a distance, they had followed Jesus from Galilee and provided everything he needed as much as they were able. Among the women were Jesus' mother Mary, Mary Magdalene, Mary the mother of James and Joseph, and the mother of the sons of Zebedee. On the night that Jesus was crucified, a rich man from Arimathea named Joseph, who was also a disciple of Jesus, went to Pilate and asked for the body of Jesus.

Joseph: My lord, I have come to ask for the body of Jesus to be buried in my own new tomb. Everything is arranged for his burial.

Pilate: So be it! My soldiers will assist you. What has happened here is a terrible thing. That man was innocent and should not have been killed. You may take his body and give him a proper burial. There is so much about the people here

I will never understand.

Narrator: So, Joseph took the body of Jesus and wrapped it in a clean linen cloth. He laid it in his own new tomb, which he had hewn in the rock. He then rolled a great stone to the door of the tomb and went away. Mary Magdalene and the other Mary were there, sitting opposite the tomb. Meanwhile, Caiaphas, the chief priests, and the Pharisees went back to Pilate.

Caiaphas: Sir, we remember what that impostor said while he was still alive, "After three days I will rise again." Therefore command the tomb to be made secure until the third day; otherwise his disciples may go and steal him away, and tell the people, "He has been raised from the dead." That last deception would be worse than the first.

Pilate: You have a guard of soldiers; go, make it as secure as you can.

Sing a congregational hymn of your choice.

BENEDICTION

Go into the World with Joy

Brothers and sisters, Jesus Christ, our Savior, is alive!

Death could not keep him away.

The grave could not hold him.

Christ is alive!

There is joy this morning!

Go into the world with joy.

There are people waiting to hear the good news.

Tell the world Christ lives.

Tell the world of God's love.

Go, my sisters and brothers, go without fear; go without shame; go without apology.

Go in the name of Jesus Christ.

Amen.

RECESSIONAL

Sing a recessional hymn of your choice. Recess from the sanctuary with Jesus leading the crowd. This is both a somber reminder of the Passion and the difficult moments in our own lives, and a joyful celebration of the new life of Easter.

ENGAGING AND RESPONDING TO THE WORD: AT THE FOOT OF THE CROSS

Leader preparation: This is a simple but powerful activity that's good to use during a season of repentance, like Lent. You'll want to think of things that keep you from being a faithful steward of God's gifts; and you'll be encouraging others to do the same thing.

Supplies:
- slips of paper
- pens or pencils
- (optional) smooth rocks and markers
- a cross

Invite someone to read aloud Isaiah 55:1–3 and another person to read Mark 10:17–22. Note that both passages call for change. Being faithful disciples and stewards often requires us to make changes in our lives. Ask the group to think of something that keeps them from being the person God calls them to be. Another possibility is to ask them to think of something that keeps their church from being the church God is calling it to be. Allow time to write these ideas on the slips of paper. Then invite all, person by person, to come before the cross to lay this obstacle to their (or the church's) growth at the foot of the cross. If markers and smooth stones are easily available, use these instead of pens or pencils and slips of paper. The rocks will signify the heaviness of the burdens they are laying down.

When everyone has laid down their "obstacles," invite the group to join in the following prayer: *Merciful God, we come to you carrying heavy burdens that we don't need to carry. We haul around obstacles that keep us from living as the disciples and stewards you call us to be.*

As we lay these at the foot of your cross, help us to let go of them. Forgive us for carrying them and help us to forgive ourselves. Freed from these burdens, may we live as the people you call us to be. We pray in the name of our Savior, who calls us to be faithful and who changes us. Amen.

REVERSE TENEBRAE (SERVICE OF LIGHTING)

Leader preparation: Pastors often like to take off the Sunday after Easter. That's an ideal time to have a "laity Sunday." In a Tenebrae service, candles are extinguished to portray the betrayal, abandonment, and agony of the events of Holy Thursday (Maundy Thursday) and Good Friday. For churches that do a Tenebrae, a service of reading and lighting candles will make sense. This serial monologue allows each of a group of seven people to write only a couple of paragraphs, and invites friends to edit the writing.

Supplies:
- Bibles
- writing materials
- eight white candles and a taper
- "Reverse Tenebrae (Service of Lighting)" script on page 93–94
- "Order of Service" on page 95–97

Invite eight people to participate in planning and writing a reverse Tenebrae or lighting service. Each person stands, reads, and lights a candle, because all the stories are about the good news after the resurrection. One person represents Cleopas, the part that is written out as a guide. The other seven people will write their parts based on the prompt in the script. Schedule an hour for the planning meeting plus a 20-minute rehearsal with taper and candles.

REVERSE TENEBRAE (SERVICE OF LIGHTING)

One model and seven prompts for writing short testimonies

Cleopas: I heard Jesus preach in the Emmaus area. I even went over to Bethany. In fact, I was there when... well, you know, when Lazarus...wasn't dead anymore. It was incredible. I wasn't important in the ministry. I was one of the Seventy, sure, and did a little teaching of the simpler concepts, but this is my story....(*Model from Luke 24:13–32.*)

Samuel and I went to see Jesus' really close friends in Jerusalem after he died to tell them how sorry we were. We were coming back from the condolence visit and scratching our heads a little at the wild story Mary told about Jesus' tomb being empty when we met this traveler who started walking with us. He was clueless about what had happened over Passover, and we told him about Jesus— how amazing he was and what a tragedy that his ministry was cut short. Miserable Romans—wouldn't know a holy man if they tripped over him!

This traveler started with the old prophets and Moses and explained how the Messiah had to suffer before there could be any glory. And while he was talking, I felt this strange glowing in my heart. Well, we got to Emmaus town limits at nightfall, and the traveler looked like he was going further, so we convinced him to stay for dinner. Now, this is the really remarkable part of my testimony. When we asked him to say the blessing and break the bread, we suddenly knew that the man was Jesus himself.

Light one candle.

Tabitha: I can't say I ever encountered Jesus of Nazareth himself. To be honest, if he had come to Joppa, I probably would have been too busy to notice. I'm Tabitha. The Greeks call me Dorcas and this is my story...(*Continue story based on Acts 9:36–43.*)

Light one candle.

Sing a song of your choice.

Ananias: When God gives you a vision with Jesus in it—well, of course it's comforting, supportive, beautiful, inspiring—right? Wrong! This is my scary story...(*Continue story based on Acts 9:1–23.*)

Light one candle.

Lydia: I have a big house and a lucrative business of selling purple, that rare and expensive dye. This is my story...(*Continue story based on Acts 16:11–15.*)

Light one candle.

Sing a song of your choice.

Philip: People are different. Their stories are different. This is the way I learned that truth...(*Continue story based on Acts 8:26–40.*)

Light one candle.

Paul: You've got my letters. I can't add much here, but maybe you'd like to hear my side of what Ananias told you... (*Continue story based on Acts 9:1–23.*)

Light one candle.

Sing a song of your choice.

Damaris *(a slave girl)*: Crazy? Yes, everyone thought I was crazy…

(Continue story based on Acts 16:16–24.)

Light one candle.

Hector *(a jailer)*: Do you know what happens to a warden if his prisoners escape? Death! This is my story…
(Continue story based on Acts 16:19–34.)

Light one candle.

Sing a song of your choice.

ORDER OF SERVICE

Gathering Words and Welcome

Opening prayer: *Gracious God, thank you for your presence with us in worship in this season of resurrection. Help us not only to hear the stories of long ago, but to respond with our own lives to your risen presence in our midst. Amen.*

Invitation to the Service of Lighting: You may have participated in a Tenebrae Service on Maundy Thursday, when the shadows grow as candles are extinguished and Jesus' arrest, trial, and crucifixion are remembered. This is a "Reverse Tenebrae"—a service of lighting—when we remember all the witnesses to Jesus' resurrected presence.

Scripture: Hebrews 11:1–3, 12:1–2

Cleopas speaks. Light one candle.

Tabitha speaks. Light one candle.

Hymn: *(Sung to the tune of "Breathe on me, Breath of God," Trentham)*
Breathe on me, Breath of God;
Light me within, without.
Wake up the dead;
speak through the bread
till hope replaces doubt.
Breathe on me, Breath of God;
teach me to be a friend
to even those who reach for me,
and be at my journey's end.
Breathe on me, Breath of God
and let this candle burn,
so any wanderer day or night
can meet you and then return.

Ananias speaks. Light one candle.

Lydia speaks. Light one candle.

Hymn: *(Sung to the tune of "Jesus Calls Us O'er the Tumult," Galilee)*
Jesus calls us, when the tumult comes from
somewhere deep inside,
calls us forth to share the gospel, helps us
leave the place we hide.
We can learn to heal each other, open
doors to the unknown.
We can risk and we can nurture sanctuary
in our homes.
Jesus calls us and we listen; Jesus asks, we
take a chance, Jesus lights us and we glimmer; Jesus meets
us and we dance.

Philip speaks. Light one candle.

Paul speaks. Light one candle.

Hymn: *(Sung to the tune of "Lord, I Want to be a Christian," Smith)*
God, I want to be like Philip,
in my heart, in my heart.
God, I want to be like Philip, in my heart.
Share the sto-ry, share the water, too!
God, I want to be a Christian, just like him.
God, I want to be like Pa-ul,
with my mind, with my mind.
God, I want to be like Pa-ul,
with my mind.
On the road. . . and the temple mount!
God, I want to be a Christian, just like him.
God, I want to be the Christian
that you need, in my time.

God, I want to be a Christian in my time!

Give me faith, hope, and love that's free!

God, I want to be a Christian, just like me.

Damaris (a slave girl) speaks. Light one candle.

Hector (a jailer) speaks. Light one candle.

Hymn: Choose a congregational favorite.

Invitation to the congregation: Philippians 1: 3–11

Closing prayer: *Risen Christ, live in us. Help us to tell our own stories of witness to your love; help us to shine a light always in our world. Amen.*

A BIBLICAL JOURNEY FOR HOLY THURSDAY AND GOOD FRIDAY: FROM TABLE TO GARDEN, CROSS TO TOMB

Leader preparation: Scripture is passed on in vivid ways through the liturgy of the church year. The story of Jesus' trial, suffering, crucifixion, and resurrection are retold in the traditional liturgies of Holy Week and Easter.

Supplies:

- (optional) meal
- decorating supplies (see options below)
- "Combined Holy Thursday and Good Friday Worship Service: From Table to Garden, Cross to Tomb" on pages 102–106

Here's an evening worship service with a meal, blending the traditional biblical texts and stories of Holy Thursday (which often focus on the Last Supper) with the stories and texts for Good Friday and Tenebrae liturgies (which focus on the death and entombment of Jesus).

Many congregations have separate services for Thursday and Friday; instead of two services, this service blends both into one—and can occur on either evening. In the service, the group is invited to move to four different stations for a time of scripture, prayer, and music. (See pages 102–106.)

THESE FOUR STATIONS INCLUDE:

Station 1: "We Join Jesus at the Table." At this station the congregation gathers around a table/tables for a simple meal and Holy Communion.

Station 2: "We Pray with Jesus in the Garden." The congregation moves from the place of the meal to a place or setting of a garden. There they hear and reflect on Jesus' prayer and time with the disciples at Gethsemane/Mount of Olives.

Station 3: "We Face Jesus: His Trial and Cross." The congregation moves from the garden to a place where they can focus on a cross.

Station 4: "We Watch as Jesus is Placed in the Tomb." The congregation moves from the cross to a place where they can focus on the tomb.

SUGGESTIONS FOR PREPARING FOR THE SERVICE:

A simple meal: Set up tables for your congregation to share a common meal. Set up as a cross or a "T" shape. A simple meal of fruit, breads, and soup or broth can be served or set up as people come to the table. Cover the tables with purple or white tablecloths. Place palm branches from the Palm Sunday service on the table. Keep lights low—and use candles.

DECORATING OR PREPARING THE STATIONS:

Station 1 can be set up in a fellowship hall or a place where food can be shared.

Station 2 is often outside the building in a garden or on a lawn.

Station 3 may focus on a cross outside or back inside the building where a cross can be seen. Sometimes a cross is constructed for the service.

Station 4 can be in the sanctuary with an image or video of a tomb projected on the wall. Such images are available through stock photo sites such as iStockphoto. (For example, see iStockphoto image "Tomb in Holy Land," #8368395 or the "Empty Tomb" continuous video clip, #9593248). During the service, there should be a large lit candle at each station that gets extinguished as people leave for the next station.

Scriptures, music, and chime/bell: If you use the Revised Common Lectionary to guide worship, adjust the gospel readings for the particular year. The various readings are included in the worship attachment. For year A, use the readings from Matthew. In year B, use readings from Mark and in year C, use the gospel of Luke.

The refrain from the Taizé song "Stay with Me" is used throughout the service as the bidding song. The congregation sings it as they move from station to station. Listen to a recording of "Stay with Me" on YouTube. If you're unable to locate the music, use the first verse of "Were You There?" as the bidding song.

In the service following each reading, there's a "song for meditation." These songs may be sung by the choir, a soloist, or the congregation. Choose appropriate songs for each reading. Songs for Holy Week are found in most hymnals. This service also suggests the song, "Come to the Table of Grace" after the reading about the Last Supper and "Were You There?" (perhaps sung as a solo without accompaniment), following the last reading in the service. As indicated in the service beginning on page 102, at the sound of a chime or bell, the group will know that a moment of silence is over. They'll also know when it's time to sing the bidding song and move to the next station.

Holy Communion/Lord's Supper: Please use the liturgy that's appropriate for your tradition. If possible, allow Holy Communion to be shared following the simple meal, seated around tables.

Readers and dancer: Invite different readers to lead the "bidding prayers" and read the scriptures. Instruct them to read slowly and clearly. Allow a time of silence following each reading. You may also invite a dancer or guide to lead the group from one station to another. In the garden, at the cross, and at the tomb, the guide or dancer may kneel in prayer during the readings. Following the silence, they may be the ones to extinguish the candle.

Removal of Bible, basin, and candles; and the conclusion of the service: Some congregations strip the sanctuary of symbols during the conclusion of a Good Friday service. They return the symbols to the sanctuary as part of one of the Easter services. In this service, the removal may be done in silence following the singing of "Were You There?" At the end of the service, offer a benediction and extinguish the final candle. As safety will allow, have the congregation leave in darkness.

COMBINED HOLY THURSDAY AND GOOD FRIDAY WORSHIP SERVICE

It's worth the journey . . .
From Table to Garden, Cross to Tomb
Stay with me, remain here with me.
Watch and pray, watch and pray.

—Taizé prayer song

GREETING AND INTRODUCTION

Christ's peace be yours this evening. This night combines traditions of Holy Thursday and Good Friday. On this night, we join Jesus in those last days around a table with his followers. We join him in a garden wondering if we can stay awake and abide with him. We will join him at his trial and witness the cross. Tonight, Jesus will be put to rest in a tomb. Silence and darkness await us. Friends, we join together as companions on this journey. May God touch us, draw us close to Christ and one another and may we be changed. God is with us.

Throughout the service when you hear the sound of the chime, we will sing together the refrain, "Stay with Me." Following our guide, we will then move together to another station on this evening's journey. Now, let us begin by greeting one another and offering the peace of God to those around us at the table.

PASSING OF THE PEACE

STATION 1: WE JOIN JESUS AT THE TABLE
BIDDING SONG *(AT THE SOUND OF THE CHIME)*
"STAY WITH ME"

GRACE *(UNISON)*

Come, Lord Jesus, be our guest.

Let these gifts to us be blest. Amen.

(attributed to Martin Luther)

A SIMPLE MEAL SHARED

BIDDING SONG *(AT THE SOUND OF THE CHIME)*
"STAY WITH ME"

BIDDING PRAYER *(UNISON)*

Christ, you call us to your table to share in your presence. Bless us as we remember that last supper with your friends. And on this night, strengthen us for the days ahead as you come once again in the sharing of bread and cup. Amen.

MT 26:17-25 / MK 14:12-21 / LK 22:1-13

Jesus prepares for the supper and predicts betrayal.

(A time of silent reflection and prayer)

CHOOSE A SONG OF MEDITATION

Have choir sing first verse and assembly sing the following.

MT 26:26-29 / MK 14:22-25 / LK 22:14-34

Jesus blesses bread and wine.

(A time of silent reflection and prayer)

HOLY COMMUNION

(All are invited to participate. Following the blessing, please pass the bread and cup to one another saying "Body of Christ" or "Cup of Blessing." Then dip bread into cup.)

STATION 2: WE PRAY WITH JESUS IN THE GARDEN
BIDDING SONG *(AT THE SOUND OF THE CHIME)*
"STAY WITH ME"

(All follow dancer to the garden.)

BIDDING PRAYER *(UNISON)*

Christ, you call us to join you in a time of prayer and testing.

Though we may leave you—sleep, betray, or flee—forgive us.

Keep us awake. Keep us faithful. Amen.

MT 26:36–46 / MK 14:26–42 / LK 22:39–45

Jesus and the disciples go to Gethsemane.

(A time of silent reflection and prayer)

CHOOSE A SONG OF MEDITATION

MT 26:47-56 / MK 14:26–42 / LK 22:46–62

Jesus is betrayed, arrested, and denied.

(A time of silent reflection and prayer)

STATION 3: WE FACE JESUS: HIS TRIAL AND CROSS
BIDDING SONG *(AT THE SOUND OF THE CHIME)*
"STAY WITH ME"

(All follow dancer to the cross.)

BIDDING PRAYER *(UNISON)*

Christ, you face conflict and the cross.

We face you and all who suffer.

Forgive our sin. Pour out your love.

Transform us. Amen.

MT 26:57, 63–66 / MK 14:53 / LK 22:66–71

Jesus is accused by religious leaders.

(A time of silent reflection and prayer)

LK 23:1–5 *(YEAR C ONLY)*

Jesus first encounters Pilate, Governor of Judea.

(A time of silent reflection and prayer)

MT 27:11–26 / MK 15:1–20 / LK 23:6–25

Jesus is tried and sentenced.

(A time of silent reflection and prayer)

LUKE 23:26-43 *(YEAR C ONLY)*

Jesus is led away and crucified alongside criminals.

(A time of silent reflection and prayer)

CHOOSE A SONG OF MEDITATION

MT 27:27-56/MK 15:21-41/LK 23:44-49

Jesus is crucified.

(A time of silent reflection and prayer)

STATION 4: WE WATCH AS JESUS IS PLACED IN THE TOMB
BIDDING SONG *(AT THE SOUND OF THE CHIME)*
"STAY WITH ME"

(All follow dancer to the tomb.)

BIDDING PRAYER *(UNISON)*

Christ, we watch as those who loved you grieve,

and wrap your body in linen.

Hopeless, they place you in a tomb and go away.

We join them even now.

So on this night, keep us constant in prayer and hope,

looking for the fulfillment of your resurrection in our day. Amen.

MATTHEW 27:55-56 *(YEAR A ONLY)*

Women were present.

MT 27:57-61 / MK 15:42-47 / LK 23:50-56

Jesus is placed in the tomb.

(A time of silent reflection and prayer)

SONG OF MEDITATION: "WERE YOU THERE?"

(A time of silent reflection and prayer)

REMOVAL OF BIBLE, BASIN AND CANDLES

BENEDICTION AND EXTINGUISHING THE LIGHT

(Please prayerfully leave the sanctuary in silence or humming "Stay with Me.")

This service was prepared by Sidney D. Fowler for Hope United Church of Christ, Alexandria, VA.

BACKWARD WORSHIP SERVICE

Leader preparation: Mark 16:1–8 is a Lectionary reading for Easter Day B and Easter Vigil ABC. Psalm 112 is a Lectionary reading for Epiphany 5A and Proper 17C/ Ordinary 22C.

Supplies:

- bulletins with the order of worship displayed in reverse order

A playful and joyful worship service sometimes grows from a change in perspective. As Christ's resurrection changed the direction for the disciples, this backward worship service can offer a fresh perspective on the new life we have in Jesus.

Reverse the order of your typical worship service, or follow this reverse template:

- Post-service Music
- Benediction
- Closing Song
- Prayer of Dedication
- Doxology
- Offering
- Prayer of Our Savior
- Pastoral Prayer
- Silent Prayers
- Joys and Concerns
- Song
- Sermon
- Bible Reading
- Children's Sermon
- Announcements
- Gloria

- Invocation
- Song
- Call to Worship
- Praise Song/Introit
- Greeting
- Welcome

RESURRECTION PRAYER LITANY

Leader preparation: In Jesus' resurrection we get a possible glimpse of the future of our bodies—what they may become like as they are raised with Christ into newness of life. This prayer will work well during the Eastertide season or on Ascension Sunday, as a reminder that our bodies are moving toward this vision of resurrection "sneak previewed" for us in the mysterious resurrection of Christ.

Supplies:

- "Resurrection Prayer Litany," page 111

Responsively pray the prayer on page 111 as part of worship. (It would work well as an opening litany.) The congregation reads the boldface parts. Alternately, you could assign the lines to various people and pray it in a reader's theater format.

RESURRECTION PRAYER LITANY

O Christ, your body rose from the grave, yet not just as any ordinary body;

You bore your distinctive scars, yet you were hard for us to recognize.

You cooked fish with us on the beach, just like always—

Then you passed through a locked door in a way we'd never witnessed.

You told us we couldn't hold on to you, only to invite us to touch your hands and side.

You promised to be with us always, only to turn around and ascend into heaven, your physical body gone from sight.

But . . . your body is still seen—it's right here, among us.

It *is us*.

For you have made us to be your body;

You have shaped us to be the fullness of you who fills everything in every way.

You promised that, though what our bodies will become has not yet been made known,

We will somehow embody your resurrected fullness.

Even now we are the mysterious, beautiful body of Christ; each one of us is part of it.

Let us grow into this new self, bringing honor to Christ's body through the way our bodies live and move and have their being. Amen.